Fitness Studio Ownership

Insights into the fitness studio industry, including business models, marketing, and operations.

Emerson Reagan

Introduction

Welcome to the world of fitness studio ownership, where passion for health and wellness merges with entrepreneurial spirit. In today's fast-paced and health-conscious society, the fitness industry plays a pivotal role, offering individuals a space to prioritize their physical and mental well-being. Within this dynamic landscape, fitness studios have emerged as trendsetters, providing a personalized and immersive fitness experience.

If you've ever dreamt of owning a fitness studio or are simply intrigued by the inner workings of this flourishing industry, you've come to the right place. This comprehensive guide will take you on a fascinating journey, shedding light on the various facets of fitness studio ownership.

The chapters ahead are designed to equip you with valuable insights into the fitness studio industry, delving into business models, marketing strategies, and the core operations that drive success. Whether you're considering launching your own fitness studio or seeking to refine an existing one, the knowledge and wisdom shared within this guide will prove invaluable.

Discover the secrets behind the dazzling growth and trends shaping the industry today. Uncover the essence of a well-structured business model, be it a boutique studio, a franchise, or an independent venture. Gain a deep understanding of the critical components involved in setting up a fitness studio: from choosing the ideal location to curating the perfect equipment and amenities.

Embark on a journey into the world of marketing strategies, where you'll uncover the power of branding, digital marketing techniques, and the unparalleled influence of referral programs. And that's not all — learn the inner workings of efficient studio operations: from class scheduling and membership management to staff training and customer retention strategies.

With this comprehensive guide in your hands, you'll enter the realm of fitness studio ownership armed with the knowledge and expertise needed to thrive. So, prepare to dive deep into this captivating industry and unlock the secrets to building a successful fitness studio. Your journey begins now.

Chapter one

Understanding the Fitness Studio Industry

1.1 Growth and Trends

The fitness industry has experienced a considerable surge in popularity in recent years, with more individuals prioritizing their health and wellness. According to a report by IBIS World, the U.S. fitness industry generates over $30 billion in revenue per annum, with an annualized growth rate of 2.9% between 2016 and 2021. The report also indicates that fitness club membership has risen steadily, with a membership penetration rate of 20% in 2016.

One of the significant trends in recent years is the rise of boutique fitness studios. These studios offer a personalized and specialized experience, often catering to niche audiences such as cyclists, dancers, or yogis. Boutique studios have carved out a unique space in the fitness industry, presenting a trendy and immersive fitness experience. These studios are often smaller in size, which facilitates a sense of community and personalized attention.

Another trend in the industry is the immense popularity of classes that incorporate group workouts and technology. Spin classes, high-intensity interval training (HIIT), and dance cardio classes have emerged as top trending workouts in recent years. These classes use technology such as heart rate monitors, virtual reality, and customized programming to personalize the experience and engage participants.

The rise of wearable fitness technology has also shaped the fitness industry's growth and trends. Wearables such as smartwatches, fitness trackers, and heart rate monitors enable individuals to track their exercise progress and quantify their fitness goals. This data visualization and tracking have enabled individuals to personalize and optimize their workout routines.

Yet another trend in the fitness industry is the convergence of technology and fitness. Fitness apps, streaming platforms, and virtual classes have made fitness accessible from anywhere at any time. This has helped break down barriers to entry, promoting inclusivity and diversity in the industry.

The changing landscape of the fitness industry has brought forth significant trends, driving the industry's growth and evolution. As we move forward, it is crucial to stay attuned to these trends and continue to innovate and personalize the fitness experience to retain a loyal customer base and drive revenue growth.

1.2 Market Analysis

Performing a thorough market analysis is crucial before venturing into the fitness studio industry. Understanding the market landscape, demographics, and competition will provide essential insights that can shape your business strategy and set you up for success.

One important aspect of market analysis is identifying your target audience. Fitness studios cater to a wide range of individuals, each with unique preferences and fitness goals. Conducting market research will help you determine the demographics and psychographics of your potential customers. Are you targeting young professionals seeking high-intensity workouts, or are you catering to older adults looking for low-impact exercises? By defining your target audience, you can tailor your offerings and marketing efforts accordingly.

Analyzing the geographical and demographic factors of your target market is also crucial. Look for areas with a concentration of your target audience, such as neighbourhoods with high-income residents or communities with a strong fitness culture. Assess the competition in those areas to identify gaps or opportunities. Are there already established fitness studios, and if so, what differentiates them? Finding a unique value proposition or a niche that is underserved can help you stand out in a crowded market.

It is also important to analyze the economic factors that may impact your fitness studio. Study the local economy's stability and growth potential, as well as any upcoming developments or trends that may influence the industry. Consider factors such as disposable income, job growth, and consumer spending patterns. A favourable economic environment can contribute to a thriving fitness studio industry, while an unstable or recession-prone market may present challenges.

Moreover, keep an eye on industry trends and innovations. Are there emerging fitness concepts or technologies that are gaining popularity? Staying up to date with industry trends can help you align your business with the changing demands and preferences of your target market.

Additionally, conduct a competitive analysis to gain insights into your competitors' strengths, weaknesses, and market positioning. Identify what sets your competition apart and think about how your fitness studio can differentiate itself. Focus on finding your unique selling points, be it specialized classes, exceptional customer service, or a distinctive atmosphere.

Remember that market analysis is an ongoing process. Monitor market trends, consumer preferences, and competition on a regular basis. Adapt your business strategies accordingly to remain relevant and competitive in the fitness studio industry. By conducting a comprehensive market analysis, you can make informed decisions and increase your chances of success in this dynamic and ever-evolving market.

1.3 Consumer Demographics

Understanding the demographics of your target audience is essential for the success of your fitness studio. By analysing consumer demographics, you can tailor your offerings, marketing strategies, and operational decisions to meet the specific needs and preferences of your customers.

One key demographic factor to consider is age. Different age groups have varying fitness goals and preferences. For example, younger individuals may be more interested in high-intensity workouts, while older adults might seek low-impact exercises or specialized programs for seniors. Analyzing the age composition of your target market will help you curate classes and programs that appeal to your intended audience.

Income level is another crucial aspect to consider. The purchasing power of your target market will impact their willingness to invest in fitness studio memberships and services. Higher-income individuals may be more inclined to spend on premium fitness experiences, while those on a tighter budget may prioritize affordability. Assessing the income levels of your target audience allows you to price your services appropriately and offer value that aligns with their financial capabilities.

Gender is another important demographic factor to consider. While fitness studios may attract a diverse customer base, certain workout styles or classes might have a higher appeal among specific genders. For example, strength training classes may attract more male participants, while dance or Pilates classes may be more popular among females. Evaluating the gender composition of your target audience will help you develop marketing strategies that resonate with their interests and preferences.

Geographical demographics also play a role in understanding your target market. Analyze the location of your fitness studio and the surrounding area to determine the population density and demographic composition. Urban areas with a younger population might have a higher demand for fitness studios, while suburban or rural areas may require a different approach. Consider the accessibility and convenience of your location for your target audience, as proximity can greatly influence their decision to join your studio.

Additionally, lifestyle and psychographic factors are essential for understanding consumer preferences. Some individuals may prioritize convenience and flexibility, seeking fitness studios with extended hours or diverse class schedules. Others may value a sense of community and social interaction, looking for studios that foster a supportive and inclusive environment. By analyzing consumer psychographics, you can design your studio's amenities, class offerings, and services to align with your target audience's preferences and lifestyles.

Conducting market research, surveys, and focus groups can help gather data on consumer demographics. This information will guide your decision-making processes, allowing you to create a fitness studio that caters to the specific needs and desires of your target market. Keep in mind that consumer demographics can change over time, so it's important to regularly reassess and adapt your strategies to remain relevant and appealing to your target audience.

Chapter two

Business Models in the Fitness Studio Industry

2.1 Boutique Studios

Boutique fitness studios have emerged as a popular business model in the fitness industry. These studios offer a unique and specialized fitness experience, catering to niche audiences with a focus on personalized attention, community, and immersive workout environments. Let's explore the key characteristics and advantages of boutique studios as a business model.

1. Specialized Offerings: Boutique studios differentiate themselves by offering specialized workout programs and classes. They often focus on specific fitness disciplines such as cycling, yoga, Pilates, barre, or high-intensity

interval training (HIIT). This specialization allows boutique studios to become experts in their chosen field, tailoring their classes and services to meet the unique needs and preferences of their target audience.

2. Personalized Attention: One of the significant advantages of boutique studios is their ability to provide personalized attention to their clients. Unlike larger gyms or fitness chains, boutique studios typically have smaller class sizes, allowing instructors to give individualized guidance and support. This personalized approach fosters a sense of community and builds strong connections between instructors and clients.

3. Immersive Environment: Boutique studios prioritize creating an immersive fitness environment that enhances the workout experience. Studios invest in high-quality equipment, sound systems, and aesthetics to create an

ambience that aligns with their brand and workout style. This attention to detail creates a unique and engaging atmosphere that adds value to the overall fitness experience.

4. Community Building: Boutique studios place a strong emphasis on building a sense of community among their clients. This is achieved through various means such as organizing social events, offering specialized workshops, and creating online platforms for clients to connect with each other. By fostering a sense of belonging and camaraderie, boutique studios create loyal and dedicated communities that keep members coming back for more.

5. Premium Pricing: Boutique studios often operate at a premium price point compared to traditional gyms or fitness chains. This is because they offer specialized services, personalized attention, and an enhanced

experience. The target audience for boutique studios is typically willing to pay a premium for the exclusive and unique offerings. The premium pricing also contributes to the perception of quality and exclusivity associated with boutique fitness studios.

6. Repeat Business and Membership Models: Boutique studios often rely on a membership model or package pricing to encourage repeat business and create a stable revenue stream. Clients can purchase memberships or class packages that offer better value compared to single-class purchases. This not only encourages loyalty but also helps studios plan and manage their capacity effectively.

7. Scalability and Expansion Opportunities: While boutique studios may start with a single location, successful ones have the potential for growth and expansion. As the fitness

industry continues to evolve, there are opportunities for boutique studios to scale their business through multiple locations, franchising, or licensing their brand and workout programs to other fitness enthusiasts.

2.2 Franchise Models

Franchise models have become a popular business model in the fitness studio industry, offering entrepreneurs an opportunity to enter the market with an established brand and proven business model. Franchising allows individuals to leverage the success and reputation of an existing fitness studio brand while operating their own business. Let's explore the key features and advantages of franchise models in the fitness studio industry.

1. Established Brand and Reputation: One of the main advantages of opting for a franchise model is the access to an established brand and reputation. Franchisees benefit

from the recognition and trust that consumers have in the franchise brand, making it easier to attract customers and establish a strong foothold in the market. The brand's existing marketing efforts and customer base can significantly contribute to the success of the franchisee's business.

2. Proven Business Model: Franchises offer a proven business model that has been tested and refined by the franchisor. This eliminates much of the trial and error that new businesses typically face. Franchisees receive comprehensive training and ongoing support from the franchisor, ensuring they have the necessary tools and knowledge to operate the business successfully. The established systems and processes provided by the franchisor help streamline operations, from marketing strategies to inventory management.

3. Operational Support and Training: Franchise models provide extensive support and training to franchisees, helping them navigate the challenges of starting and running a fitness studio. Franchisors often offer initial training programs, ongoing coaching, and access to resources such as marketing materials and operational manuals. This support allows franchisees to benefit from the expertise and experience of the franchisor, increasing their chances of success and reducing the risks associated with starting a new business.

4. Economies of Scale: Franchise models benefit from economies of scale, which can lead to cost savings for franchisees. The franchisor's purchasing power allows them to negotiate favourable rates for equipment, supplies, and other operational needs, reducing the overall expenses for franchisees. Additionally, shared marketing efforts across the franchise network can be more

cost-effective compared to individual marketing campaigns, allowing franchisees to benefit from brand recognition without significant marketing costs.

5. Brand Consistency and Standardization: Franchise models ensure brand consistency and standardization across all franchise locations. Franchisees follow predetermined guidelines for everything from facility design to customer service, ensuring a consistent experience for customers regardless of the location they visit. This standardized approach not only helps maintain the reputation of the brand but also simplifies the training and management processes for franchisees.

6. Quick Market Entry: Starting a business from scratch can be time-consuming and challenging. Franchise models offer a faster market entry for entrepreneurs looking to establish a fitness studio. With an established brand and

business model, franchisees can avoid the extensive research, planning, and development stages associated with starting a new business. This allows them to enter the market more quickly and start generating revenue sooner.

7. Growth and Expansion Opportunities: Franchise models provide franchisees with the opportunity for growth and expansion. Franchisees can leverage the success of their initial location to open additional franchise locations in new markets. This scalability allows them to capitalize on the brand's reputation and customer base, ultimately increasing their revenue and market presence.

While franchise models in the fitness studio industry offer numerous advantages, it's important for prospective franchisees to carefully evaluate the terms and conditions before committing to a franchise agreement. Franchise fees, ongoing royalties, and territorial restrictions are some factors that need to be considered. Conducting thorough research, consulting with professionals, and speaking with existing franchisees can help ensure a successful and mutually beneficial franchise partnership.

2.3 Independent Studios

Independent studios are an alternative business model in the fitness studio industry, offering entrepreneurs the opportunity to create their own unique brand and vision. These studios operate outside of established franchise systems, allowing owners to have full creative control and flexibility over their business. Let's explore the key characteristics and advantages of independent studios in the fitness studio industry.

1. Creative Freedom: One of the main advantages of independent studios is the ability to exercise creative freedom. Owners have the freedom to design their studio

space, create their own workout programs and class schedules, and develop a unique brand identity. This flexibility allows owners to tailor their offerings to their target audience's preferences and differentiate themselves from competitors.

2. Flexibility in Business Practices: Independent studios have the advantage of being able to adapt and change their business practices quickly. Owners can experiment with different pricing models, class formats, marketing strategies, and partnerships without the constraints of a franchise agreement. This flexibility allows owners to be responsive to market trends and customer demands, making it easier to pivot and continuously improve their business.

3. Personalized Customer Experience: Independent studios often excel in providing a personalized customer

experience. With a smaller, more intimate setting, owners and instructors can build strong relationships with their clients. They can offer tailored guidance and support, understand and address individual needs, and create a sense of community among clients. This personalized approach fosters loyalty and customer retention.

4. Brand Differentiation: Independent studios have the opportunity to develop a unique brand and position themselves as a distinct offering in the market. By focusing on a specific niche, offering a specialized workout program, or emphasizing a particular approach to fitness, independent studios can stand out from larger, more generalized fitness chains. This differentiation allows them to attract a specific target audience and build a loyal customer base.

5. Entrepreneurial Spirit and Control: Independent studio owners have the satisfaction of building something from scratch and being in control of their business. They can make decisions independently, from hiring and training staff to selecting equipment and designing the studio space. This entrepreneurial spirit allows owners to fully invest themselves in their vision and create a fitness studio that reflects their passions and values.

6. Greater Profit Margins: Operating an independent studio can potentially lead to higher profit margins compared to franchise models. Without the ongoing fees and royalties associated with franchises, independent studio owners can allocate more revenue towards business growth, marketing efforts, and facility improvements. This financial independence allows owners to have more control over their long-term profitability and sustainability.

7. Innovative and Adaptive: Independent studios often have the advantage of being more nimble and innovative compared to larger, established fitness chains. They can quickly adapt to changing trends and implement new workout styles or equipment. Independent studios can also experiment with unique class formats, collaborations with local businesses, and partnerships to create a dynamic and evolving fitness experience for their clients.

While independent studios offer numerous advantages, it's important to consider the challenges that come with operating without the support and resources provided by franchises. Independent studio owners may need to invest more time and effort into marketing, branding, and business development. They also bear full responsibility for financial stability and growth. However, with careful planning, strategic decision-making, and a strong entrepreneurial spirit, independent studios can thrive and become successful players in the fitness studio industry.

Chapter three

Setting Up a Fitness Studio

3.1 Location and Space Considerations

When setting up a fitness studio, one of the most critical decisions is choosing the right location and considering space requirements. The location and space of a fitness studio can significantly impact its success, accessibility, and overall customer experience. Let's explore the key considerations when it comes to location and space for a fitness studio.

1. Demographics and Target Market: Understanding the demographics of the target market is crucial when selecting a location for a fitness studio. Consider factors such as age, income level, and lifestyle preferences. For

example, if the target market consists of busy professionals, locating the studio near offices or residential areas might be ideal. Conducting market research and analyzing competitor locations can help identify areas with high demand and minimal competition.

2. Accessibility and Convenience: The location of a fitness studio should be easily accessible to the target market. Consider factors such as proximity to public transportation, major roads, and parking availability. Choosing a location that is convenient for clients to reach, especially during peak hours, can significantly impact the studio's customer base and retention rates.

3. Foot Traffic and Visibility: A visible location can attract potential customers who might be passing by. High foot traffic areas, such as shopping malls, busy streets, or popular neighbourhoods, can provide exposure to a larger

audience. Being located in a visible and easily recognizable space can generate interest and draw in potential customers who were previously unaware of the studio's existence.

4. Size and Layout: The size and layout of the space should align with the fitness studio's intended offerings and the number of clients it aims to accommodate. Consider the number of workout areas, the size of each area, and the availability of additional spaces for amenities such as locker rooms, showers, and waiting areas. It is essential to have sufficient space for clients to move comfortably during workouts and for instructors to conduct classes effectively.

5. Safety and Compliance: When selecting a location, it is crucial to ensure that the space meets all necessary safety and compliance regulations. This includes factors such as building codes, fire safety codes, accessibility regulations,

and zoning restrictions. Consulting with professionals, such as architects and attorneys, can help navigate these requirements and ensure the space meets all necessary standards.

6. Noise and Environmental Considerations: Fitness studios often generate noise, especially during high-intensity workouts or classes with loud music. Choosing a location that minimizes potential noise disruptions to neighbouring businesses or residential areas is important to maintain good relationships with the surrounding community. Additionally, considering the environmental elements, such as adequate ventilation and natural light, can enhance the overall workout experience for clients.

7. Cost and Lease Terms: The cost and lease terms of a location are crucial factors to consider when setting up a

fitness studio. It's important to conduct a thorough financial analysis to ensure the business can sustain the rent or mortgage payments along with other expenses. Negotiating favourable lease terms, such as rent escalations and renewal options, can provide stability and flexibility for the long-term success of the fitness studio.

8. Future Growth Potential: While starting with a location that fulfils the immediate needs of the fitness studio is important, considering the future growth potential is also crucial. Assessing the scalability of the space and the potential for expanding or adding additional locations can help plan for long-term growth and prevent the need for relocation in the future.

3.2 Equipment and Amenities

When setting up a fitness studio, selecting the right equipment and amenities is crucial to creating an optimal workout environment that will attract and retain clients. The right equipment and amenities can elevate your studio and differentiate it from competitors, creating a loyal following of fitness enthusiasts. In this section, we will explore the key equipment and amenities that are essential for setting up a successful fitness studio.

1. Cardio Equipment

   Cardio is a vital component of any effective workout routine, and choosing the right equipment is important. Common cardio equipment includes treadmills, ellipticals, rowing machines, and stationary bikes. These machines allow clients to get their heart rate up and burn calories efficiently. Make sure to invest in high-quality equipment that will last a long time and doesn't require frequent maintenance. In addition, consider providing equipment that helps clients track their progress such as heart rate monitors that can sync with the equipment.

2. Strength Training Equipment

Strength training is just as important as cardio, and therefore creating a space with the proper strength training equipment is necessary. Popular strength training equipment includes dumbbells, barbells, kettlebells, resistance bands, and weight machines. Having a wide array of equipment available will accommodate different fitness levels and goals. Consider offering group fitness classes that focus on strength as clients might motivate each other and learn proper form.

3. Functional Training Equipment

   Functional training is becoming increasingly popular due to its ability to work multiple muscle groups simultaneously. Popular functional training equipment includes battling ropes, TRX suspension, sandbags, and stability balls. Functional training designs help clients mimic real-life movements, which results in an improved range of motion.

4. Amenities

   Providing amenities can help differentiate your studio and create a desirable environment. An excellent way to set your workout space apart is by keeping it clean and tidy. Clients appreciate a clean atmosphere and are likelier to come back. Additionally, consider amenities such as locker rooms, shower facilities, and towel service. These small amenities can make clients feel more comfortable and encourage them to return regularly. Consider providing water and healthy snacking options to satisfy the client's nutritional needs too.

5. Lighting and Sound

The atmosphere you create in your fitness studio can be vital to creating a welcoming and energizing environment. Lighting is an essential aspect of that atmosphere and can improve the ambience of your space. A well-lit interior will set the tone and encourage clients to push further. As for sound, provide a playlist that vibes with the workout class or allows clients to listen to personal playlists. Well-curated music and proper surround sound will create a memorable experience.

3.3 Staffing and HR

When setting up a fitness studio, staffing and human resources (HR) play a vital role in ensuring the smooth operation and success of the business. Building a strong team of qualified and dedicated professionals can contribute to creating a positive and effective environment for both staff and clients. Let's explore the key considerations when it comes to staffing and HR for a fitness studio.

1. Define Staff Roles and Qualifications: Begin by identifying the specific roles and positions that need to be filled in the fitness studio. Common staff roles may include fitness instructors, personal trainers, front desk receptionists, and maintenance personnel. Clearly define the qualifications, certifications, and experience required for each role to ensure that the staff members are qualified to meet the needs of the studio and its clients.

2. Recruitment and Hiring Process: Developing an effective recruitment and hiring process is essential to attract and select the most suitable candidates for the fitness studio. Consider advertising job openings on relevant platforms, such as fitness industry job boards or local community boards. Implement a thorough screening process, including reviewing resumes, conducting interviews, and checking references. It's also important to assess each candidate's compatibility with the studio culture and their ability to align with the studio's mission and values.

3. Training and Development Programs: Providing comprehensive training and development programs is crucial for building a skilled and knowledgeable team. Invest in initial onboarding and orientation to familiarize new hires with the studio's policies, procedures, and expectations. Ongoing training opportunities, such as

workshops, certification programs, and continuing education courses, can help staff members stay updated with industry trends and enhance their expertise. This investment in training contributes to the professional growth of the staff and ensures a high standard of service for clients.

4. Employee Engagement and Retention: Fostering a positive and engaging work environment is key to staff satisfaction and retention. Implement strategies to boost employee morale, such as recognition programs, team-building activities, and regular communication channels. Actively seek feedback from staff members and address their concerns or suggestions. Providing opportunities for career advancement and professional growth within the studio can also contribute to employee retention and loyalty.

5. Compensation and Benefits: Developing a competitive compensation and benefits package is crucial for attracting and retaining top talent. Research industry standards and consider offering benefits such as health insurance, retirement plans, fitness memberships, and performance-based incentives. Ensuring fair and competitive compensation demonstrates the studio's commitment to valuing and rewarding its staff members.

6. Policies and Procedures: Establishing clear policies and procedures is essential for maintaining consistency and professionalism within the fitness studio. Develop a comprehensive staff handbook that covers aspects such as attendance, dress code, code of conduct, client interaction guidelines, and studio policies. Regularly review and update these policies to adapt to changing circumstances and ensure compliance with legal requirements.

7. Performance Evaluation and Feedback: Implementing a formal performance evaluation process helps monitor staff performance, identify strengths and areas for improvement, and provide constructive feedback. Conduct regular evaluations, set goals, and provide performance-based incentives to motivate and reward staff members. Encourage open and ongoing communication to address any concerns or issues promptly.

8. Compliance with Employment Laws: Compliance with relevant employment laws and regulations is crucial to protect the rights of both the fitness studio and its staff. Familiarize yourself with laws related to minimum wage, employment contracts, working hours, and benefits entitlement. It's advisable to consult with legal professionals or HR experts to ensure compliance and avoid any potential legal issues.

Chapter four

Marketing Strategies for Fitness Studios

4.1 Branding and Positioning

Branding and positioning are crucial elements of marketing strategies for fitness studios. Effective branding and positioning allow a fitness studio to stand out in a competitive market and attract and retain clients. Let's explore the key considerations when it comes to branding and positioning for marketing strategies of fitness studios.

1. Defining the Studio's Brand Identity: Begin by defining the fitness studio's brand identity. This includes the studio's name, logo, colours, tone of voice, and overall aesthetic. The brand identity should reflect the studio's mission, values, and unique selling proposition. Consider the target

market when developing the brand identity, as it should resonate with the studio's ideal clients.

2. Establishing a Strong Positioning Strategy: Develop a strong positioning strategy that differentiates the fitness studio from competitors and appeals to the target market. Consider the studio's strengths and unique offerings and communicate them effectively in all marketing materials. Positioning the fitness studio as an expert in a particular type of training or focusing on a specific niche can help attract a dedicated following of clients.

3. Creating a Consistent Brand Experience: Consistency is key in building a recognizable and reputable brand. Ensure that the brand identity is consistent across all touchpoints, including social media, website, print materials, and in-studio experience. This includes using consistent

messaging, imagery, and visual elements to enhance brand recognition and recall.

4. Utilizing the Power of Social Media: Social media is a powerful tool for building brand awareness, engaging with clients, and promoting the fitness studio's unique offerings. Develop a social media strategy that aligns with the brand identity and target market. Utilize social media platforms such as Instagram, Facebook, and YouTube to showcase the studio's workouts, trainers, classes, and achievements.

5. Partnering with Influencers and Sponsors: Partnering with influencers and sponsors can be a powerful strategy for building brand awareness and credibility. Consider reaching out to local influencers or industry leaders to promote the studio's offerings, or consider sponsoring community events or sports teams to increase the studio's visibility.

6. Investing in Professional Photography and Videography: High-quality photography and videography can enhance the studio's brand identity and provide visual content for marketing materials. Invest in professional photography and videography to showcase the studio's unique offerings and create engaging social media posts, website content, and advertising.

7. Maintaining a Strong Online Presence: A strong online presence is crucial for building and maintaining a reputable brand in today's digital age. Ensure that the fitness studio has a well-designed website that reflects the brand identity and provides essential information about the studio's offerings, classes, and trainers. Additionally, maintain accurate and up-to-date listings on directory sites such as Google My Business and Yelp to enhance online visibility and credibility.

8. Measuring Brand Performance: Finally, it's essential to measure the studio's brand performance regularly. Implement key performance indicators (KPIs) to assess the success of branding and positioning strategies, such as engagement rates on social media, website traffic, and conversion rates. Utilize this data to adjust and optimize strategies for maximum impact and effective ROIs.

4.2 Digital Marketing

Digital marketing is a valuable and increasingly essential marketing strategy for fitness studios. It allows for precise targeting of potential clients and provides opportunities for engaging and nurturing existing clients. Let's explore the key elements and considerations when it comes to digital marketing for fitness studios.

1. Defining the Target Audience: The first step in effective digital marketing for fitness studios is defining the target audience. Consider factors such as demographics, income, fitness goals, and location to develop a clear understanding of the ideal clients. This knowledge is essential in crafting digital marketing strategies that resonate with the target audience and increase the likelihood of conversion.

2. Developing a Website: Developing a website that reflects the studio's brand identity, offerings, and class schedules is crucial in digital marketing. Ensure that the website is mobile-friendly, easy to navigate, and optimized for search engines. Additionally, consider incorporating lead-capture forms to gather contact information for potential clients.

3. Implementing Search Engine Optimization (SEO): SEO is the process of optimizing a website's content, architecture, and metadata to rank higher in search engine results when potential clients search for relevant keywords. Implementing SEO boosts the website's visibility, drives traffic, and increases the likelihood of conversion.

4. Utilizing Email Marketing: Email marketing is a cost-effective and powerful tool for engaging and nurturing existing clients. Develop targeted and personalised email campaigns to promote new classes, events, and promotions. Additionally, consider incorporating a referral program to incentivize existing clients to refer their friends.

5. Creating Engaging Content: Creating engaging and informative content is a key element of digital marketing for fitness studios. Develop content such as blog posts, videos, and social media posts that provide value to the

target audience and showcase the studio's expertise and unique offerings.

6. Leveraging Social Media: Social media platforms such as Facebook, Instagram, and Twitter can be powerful tools for digital marketing for fitness studios. Develop a social media strategy that aligns with the studio's brand identity and target audience. Utilize platforms to showcase workouts, trainers, classes, events, and promotions and engage with clients through comments, messaging, and live streams.

7. Developing Paid Advertising Campaigns: Developing targeted paid advertising campaigns on social media and Google can increase the visibility and reach of the fitness studio to potential clients. Develop campaigns with clear calls-to-action and optimized targeting parameters to maximize the effectiveness of the advertising spend.

8. Measuring Digital Marketing Performance: Measuring the performance of digital marketing efforts is crucial to optimize and adjust strategies for maximum effectiveness. Implement performance tracking metrics such as website traffic, conversion rates, engagement rates, and click-through rates. Utilize this data to adjust and optimize strategies for optimal ROI.

4.3 Referral Programs and Word-of-Mouth

Referral programs and word-of-mouth marketing are highly effective marketing strategies for fitness studios. Leveraging the power of satisfied clients to spread the word about the studio can attract new clients and build a strong and loyal client base. Let's dive into the key elements and considerations when it comes to referral programs and word-of-mouth marketing for fitness studios.

1. Designing an Incentivized Referral Program: An incentivized referral program encourages existing clients to refer their friends, family, and colleagues to the fitness studio. Offer incentives such as discounted classes, free merchandise, or exclusive access to events or workouts. Clearly communicate the program details to existing clients and provide them with the necessary tools to easily refer others, such as referral cards or unique referral links.

2. Providing Exceptional Client Experiences: The foundation of a successful referral program and word-of-mouth marketing is consistently providing exceptional client experiences. From the moment a client enters the studio to their post-workout interactions, prioritize customer service, attentiveness, and personalized attention. Happy clients are more likely to recommend the studio to others.

3. Creating Shareable Content and Experiences: Develop content and experiences that clients will be excited to share with others. This can include photos and videos of engaging workouts, success stories of clients achieving their fitness goals, or special events and challenges. Encourage clients to share their experiences on social media platforms and provide them with branded hashtags to increase visibility and reach.

4. Encouraging Online Reviews: Positive online reviews play a crucial role in a fitness studio's reputation and potential for attracting new clients. Encourage existing clients to leave reviews on platforms such as Google, Yelp, and Facebook. Provide clear instructions and make the process as seamless as possible by incorporating links and reminders in post-workout emails or on the studio's website.

5. Partnering with Influencers and Brand Advocates: Collaborating with influencers and brand advocates in the fitness industry can amplify the impact of referral programs and word-of-mouth marketing. Identify influential individuals with a strong presence in the target market and consider offering them incentives for promoting the studio to their followers. This can include guest appearances, exclusive workouts, or free memberships.

6. Hosting Client Appreciation Events: Hosting client appreciation events can strengthen relationships with existing clients and encourage them to speak positively about the studio to others. Organize special workouts, workshops, or social gatherings exclusively for current clients. These events not only provide an opportunity to express gratitude but also create a space for clients to connect and share their positive experiences with others.

7. Leveraging Social Media Advocacy: Actively engage with clients on social media and develop a community where they can connect and share their experiences with one another. Encourage clients to tag the studio in their posts and stories and feature exceptional client content on the studio's official social media accounts. This social media advocacy boosts word-of-mouth marketing and extends the reach of the studio's online presence.

8. Tracking and Rewarding Referrals: Implement a system for tracking referred clients and ensure proper attribution to the referring client. This enables the studio to reward and acknowledge clients who generate referrals, which further incentivizes them to continue advocating for the studio. Consider offering tiered rewards based on the number of successful referrals made.

Chapter five

Operations and Management of a Fitness Studio

5.1 Class Scheduling and Booking

Effective class scheduling and booking systems are essential for the smooth operations and management of a fitness studio. Providing a seamless and convenient experience for both clients and staff ensures optimal utilization of resources and maximizes client satisfaction. Let's explore the key elements and considerations when it comes to class scheduling and booking for a fitness studio.

1. Diverse Class Schedule: A well-rounded and diverse class schedule is crucial to cater to the preferences and

needs of different clients. Offer a variety of classes that encompass different fitness levels, workout styles, and time slots. This allows clients to choose classes that align with their goals and preferences, increasing attendance and client retention.

2. Mindful Studio Capacity: Consider the maximum capacity of the studio when scheduling classes to ensure a comfortable and safe environment for clients. Take into account the size of the studio, equipment availability, and instructor availability when determining class capacity. Maintaining an appropriate client-to-instructor ratio fosters a positive experience and allows for personalized attention.

3. Online Class Booking System: Implementing an online class booking system streamlines the process for both clients and staff. Offer a user-friendly online platform where clients can view the class schedule, reserve spots, and

make payments. This allows for convenient access and increases client satisfaction. Additionally, the booking system should integrate with the studio's website and mobile app for a seamless user experience.

4. Waitlist Management: In situations where classes reach maximum capacity, a waitlist management system can be beneficial. Allow clients to join a waitlist for fully-booked classes, and if a spot becomes available due to a cancellation, automatically notify the first person on the waitlist. This ensures efficient utilization of class spots and reduces client frustration.

5. Class Cancellation Policy: Establish a clear and fair class cancellation policy to avoid no-shows and maximize class attendance. Communicate the policy to clients during the booking process and provide reminders through email or SMS notifications. Consider implementing a late

cancellation penalty to discourage last-minute cancellations and free up spots for other clients.

6. Cross-Class Promotion: Cross-class promotion is an effective strategy to encourage clients to try different classes offered by the fitness studio. Offer incentives such as discounted rates or loyalty rewards for clients who attend classes outside their regular routine. This increases class attendance across different offerings and maximizes the utilization of resources.

7. Staff Scheduling and Availability: Efficient staff scheduling is crucial to ensure that classes have qualified instructors and trainers available. Consider factors such as availability, expertise, and certifications when scheduling staff members. Utilize scheduling software that allows for easy communication and coordination between staff

members to avoid scheduling conflicts and ensure seamless operations.

8. Analytics and Data Tracking: Implementing an analytics and data tracking system allows the fitness studio to monitor class attendance, client preferences, and overall performance. Analyzing this data provides insights into popular classes, peak times, and underutilized time slots. This information can guide future class scheduling decisions and help optimize the studio's offerings for maximum revenue and client satisfaction.

9. Client Feedback and Surveys: Regularly seek client feedback and insights through surveys or feedback forms. This allows the studio to gauge client satisfaction, gather suggestions for class improvements, and identify areas of opportunity. Actively listen to the clients' needs and adapt

the class schedule accordingly to better serve their preferences.

10. Continuous Evaluation and Review: Class scheduling and booking systems should be subject to continuous evaluation and review to ensure effectiveness and adapt to changing client needs. Regularly assess class attendance, feedback, and industry trends to make data-driven decisions and optimize the class schedule. This fosters a dynamic and responsive approach to class scheduling that aligns with client demand.

5.2 Membership Management

Effective membership management is crucial for the operations and management of a fitness studio. From onboarding new members to retaining existing ones, a well-structured and efficient membership management system ensures smooth operations, maximizes revenue, and enhances the overall member experience. Let's delve into the key elements and considerations when it comes to membership management for a fitness studio.

1. Streamlined Onboarding Process: Develop a streamlined and user-friendly onboarding process to welcome new members to the fitness studio. This process should include easy registration, membership agreement signing, and payment options. Provide a comprehensive orientation session to familiarize new members with the facility, policies, and services to ensure a positive start to their fitness journey.

2. Membership Tiers and Options: Offer a range of membership tiers and options to cater to different client needs and preferences. This can include options for different durations, access to specific classes or facilities, and additional perks such as discounts on merchandise or

personal training sessions. Align membership offerings with target market demographics and regularly evaluate their relevance to maintain competitiveness in the fitness industry.

3. Effective Membership Renewal: Implement a structured membership renewal process to promote member retention. Several strategies can be employed, including offering incentives for early renewal, providing flexible payment plans, and sending timely and personalized reminders to members. Regular communication and engagement with members play a vital role in encouraging them to renew their memberships.

4. Member Communication and Support: Establish clear channels of communication for members to seek assistance and receive important updates. This can include a dedicated member portal on the fitness studio's

website or a mobile app, email newsletters, and social media groups or forums. Promptly respond to member inquiries and address their concerns to foster a strong sense of community and ensure member satisfaction.

5. Membership Freeze or Cancellation Policies: Develop clear policies and guidelines for membership freezes or cancellations to accommodate members' changing circumstances. Establish reasonable freeze or cancellation periods and clearly communicate the process to members. Providing transparency and flexibility in these matters helps build trust with members and increases their loyalty to the fitness studio.

6. Automated Billing and Payment: Implement an automated billing and payment system to streamline financial transactions and reduce administrative burden. An integrated system that handles recurring monthly

membership fees, additional charges, and member purchases simplifies the financial management process. Offer a variety of payment options, including credit cards, direct debit, and online payment gateways, to accommodate member preferences.

7. Membership Analytics and Reporting: Utilize membership analytics and reporting tools to gain insights into member behaviour, engagement, and performance. Track member attendance, class preferences, and engagement with studio offerings. This data can guide decisions on class scheduling, facility utilization, and targeted marketing campaigns to optimize member satisfaction and overall profitability.

8. Member Retention Programs: Develop member retention programs to actively engage and reward loyal members. Offer exclusive benefits, referral incentives,

loyalty rewards, and access to member-only events or workshops. Regularly communicate with members to share updates, offer challenges or incentives, and provide tips for maintaining fitness goals. These retention programs demonstrate the studio's commitment to member success and build long-term loyalty.

9. Upselling and Cross-Selling Opportunities: Identify upselling and cross-selling opportunities within the membership management process. Promote add-on services, personal training sessions, or merchandise at the point of sale or during member interactions. Personalize recommendations based on member preferences and goals to increase revenue while providing valuable options to enhance their fitness journey.

10. Member Feedback and Satisfaction Surveys: Regularly gather member feedback and conduct satisfaction surveys

to evaluate the effectiveness of membership management efforts. Analyze feedback to identify areas for improvement and implement necessary changes in services or policies. Addressing member concerns and actively incorporating their suggestions enhances member satisfaction and strengthens the studio's reputation.

5.3 Staff Training and Development

Staff training and development play a significant role in the operations and management of a fitness studio. Investing in the growth and professional development of staff members not only enhances the quality of services but also contributes to employee satisfaction and retention. Let's explore the key elements and considerations when it comes to staff training and development for a fitness studio.

1. Comprehensive Onboarding Program: Develop a comprehensive onboarding program to ensure new staff members are properly trained and acclimated to the fitness studio's culture and policies. This program should cover essential topics such as facility orientation, customer service training, and an introduction to studio equipment and procedures. Providing a solid foundation from the beginning sets the tone for ongoing training and development.

2. Continuing Education and Certifications: Support staff members in pursuing continuing education opportunities and acquiring relevant certifications. Encourage participation in fitness industry conferences, workshops, webinars, and seminars to stay updated on the latest trends, techniques, and research. Support financially or provide resources for staff members to obtain certifications

such as personal training, group fitness instruction, or specialized modalities.

3. In-House Training Programs: Develop in-house training programs tailored to the specific needs and goals of the fitness studio. Offer regular training sessions that cover topics such as new class formats, workout techniques, customer service skills, and studio policies and procedures. These training sessions can be led by internal experts or external professionals and should provide opportunities for hands-on practice and feedback.

4. Ongoing Skill Development: Foster a culture of ongoing skill development among staff members. Encourage them to continually improve their teaching or training techniques, communication skills, and leadership abilities. Provide resources such as books, online courses, or access to

industry experts to support staff members in their continuous learning journey.

5. Mentoring and Coaching: Establish mentorship and coaching programs to provide individualized support to staff members. Pair experienced trainers or instructors with new or less experienced staff members to provide guidance, share best practices, and foster professional growth. Regular coaching sessions can help identify areas for improvement and create action plans for skill development.

6. Cross-Training Opportunities: Provide cross-training opportunities for staff members to broaden their skill sets. Encourage trainers or instructors to learn and teach different class formats, allowing them to expand their expertise and increase their versatility. This not only enhances the studio's ability to offer diverse class options

but also provides professional growth opportunities for staff members.

7. Performance Assessments and Feedback: Conduct regular performance assessments to evaluate staff members' competencies and provide valuable feedback. Use objective criteria to assess performance and address both strengths and areas for improvement. Schedule regular feedback sessions to discuss progress, set goals, and offer support for skill development.

8. Leadership Development: Identify staff members with leadership potential and provide opportunities for their development. Offer leadership training programs, mentorship from senior management, and opportunities to lead team meetings or workshops. Nurturing and promoting internal talent contribute to a positive work

culture and facilitate the long-term growth and success of the fitness studio.

9. Recognition and Rewards: Recognize and reward staff members for their achievements, efforts, and contributions. Establish a recognition program that acknowledges outstanding performance, professionalism, and dedication. This can include awards, bonuses, public recognition, or other incentives to motivate and retain top-performing staff members.

10. Staff Surveys and Feedback: Regularly solicit staff feedback through surveys or feedback sessions to assess their satisfaction, engagement, and development needs. Actively listen to their concerns, suggestions, and ideas for improvement. Incorporate their feedback into the training and development initiatives to ensure they align with staff needs and expectations.

5.4 Customer Retention Strategies

Customer retention is a crucial aspect of the operations and management of a fitness studio. It is more cost-effective to retain existing customers than to constantly acquire new ones. Implementing effective customer retention strategies not only ensures a stable revenue stream but also fosters a loyal and engaged community. Let's explore the key elements and considerations when it comes to customer retention strategies for a fitness studio.

1. Personalized Member Experience: Provide a personalized and tailored experience to each member. Get to know their fitness goals, preferences, and challenges, and use this information to customize their workouts, classes, and overall experience. Show genuine interest in their progress and make them feel valued as individuals,

which enhances their sense of belonging and encourages long-term commitment.

2. Exceptional Customer Service: Deliver exceptional customer service at every interaction with members. Train staff members to be knowledgeable, helpful, and attentive to member needs. Promptly address member inquiries or concerns and go the extra mile to exceed their expectations. Cultivating a positive and supportive environment brings members back and earns their loyalty.

3. Regular Communication: Maintain regular communication with members to keep them engaged and updated. Send personalized emails, newsletters, or text messages to share information about upcoming events, new classes, or promotions. Seek feedback through surveys or focus groups to demonstrate that their opinions are valued and to identify areas for improvement.

4. Membership Benefits and Rewards: Offer exclusive membership benefits and rewards to incentivize members to stay active and committed. This can include discounts on retail products, priority class registration, referral rewards, or access to special events. Regularly communicate these benefits to members, ensuring they are aware of the additional value they receive as part of their membership.

5. Member Appreciation Events: Organize member appreciation events to show gratitude and foster a sense of community. This can include social gatherings, fitness challenges or competitions, workshops, or member-only classes. Such events provide opportunities for members to connect with each other and with staff, strengthening their loyalty and commitment.

6. Progress Tracking and Goal Setting: Assist members in tracking their progress and setting new goals. Offer tools such as mobile apps or online platforms that allow members to log their workouts, track their achievements, and monitor their progress. Celebrate their milestones and provide support and guidance in setting new goals to keep them engaged and motivated.

7. Continual Program Enhancement: Continually enhance and evolve fitness programs and class offerings based on member feedback and industry trends. Introduce new class formats, incorporate popular fitness trends, or add specialized workshops to cater to a variety of member interests and preferences. Offering a variety of options keeps members engaged and interested in continuing their fitness journey at the studio.

8. Retention-focused Marketing and Promotions: Develop marketing and promotional strategies that focus on member retention rather than solely on acquiring new members. Offer renewal incentives, loyalty discounts, or special offers exclusively for current members. Emphasize the ongoing value they receive from their membership and highlight success stories and testimonials from long-term members.

9. Social Media Engagement: Leverage the power of social media to engage with members and promote a sense of community. Encourage members to share their fitness journey, successes, or challenges on social media platforms using hashtags or tags associated with the studio. Engage with members by liking, commenting, or sharing their posts, creating a strong rapport and reinforcing their connection to the studio.

10. Proactive Member Feedback and Issue Resolution: Regularly seek member feedback and proactively address any issues or concerns they may have. Implement a system for members to provide feedback, whether through suggestion boxes, online surveys, or open communication channels. Promptly respond to feedback and resolve any issues to show members that their satisfaction and well-being are paramount.

By implementing these customer retention strategies, fitness studio owners can create a supportive and engaging environment that fosters member loyalty and long-term commitment. Personalizing the member experience, providing exceptional customer service, maintaining regular communication, offering membership benefits and rewards, organizing member appreciation events, assisting with progress tracking and goal setting, continually enhancing program offerings, focusing on member retention in marketing efforts, leveraging social media engagement, and proactively seeking member feedback contribute to the overall success and sustainability of the fitness studio.

Conclusion

In conclusion, fitness studio ownership encompasses a diverse range of elements that require careful consideration and strategic planning. Understanding the unique dynamics of the fitness studio industry, including business models, marketing strategies, and day-to-day operations, is crucial for success in this competitive market.

When it comes to choosing the right business model, fitness studio owners have various options to consider. Whether it's a boutique studio specializing in a specific fitness niche, a multi-discipline studio offering a variety of classes, or a hybrid model combining in-person and online offerings, selecting the right format is essential. It's important to assess market demand, target audience preferences, and competitive landscape when determining the optimal business model for the fitness studio.

Effective marketing strategies are paramount for attracting and retaining customers. Utilizing a multi-channel approach with a focus on digital platforms, such as social media, website optimization, and online advertising, can help reach a wider audience. Leveraging social proof, such as testimonials and success stories, and utilizing influencer partnerships or local collaborations, can help build credibility and trust in the community. Offering promotional incentives, referral programs, and exclusive perks for existing members can contribute to customer acquisition and retention.

In terms of operations, meticulous planning is necessary to ensure the smooth functioning of the fitness studio. Securing appropriate facilities, equipment, and staffing, as well as complying with regulatory requirements, are fundamental aspects. Investing in high-quality equipment and technology solutions can enhance the member experience and streamline administrative tasks. Implementing robust scheduling systems, booking platforms, and member management software can optimize operations and provide a seamless experience for both staff and members.

Managing the studio's finances is crucial for long-term sustainability. Establishing a solid budget, tracking expenses, and maintaining accurate financial records are essential practices. Regularly assessing the financial performance of the studio through key performance indicators, such as revenue, member retention rates, and profitability, can help identify areas for improvement and inform strategic decision-making.

Customer satisfaction and retention are paramount for sustained success in the fitness studio industry. Providing exceptional customer service, personalized experiences, and a sense of community are fundamental factors in satisfying members and fostering their loyalty. Prioritizing ongoing training and development for staff members ensures the delivery of high-quality services and a positive member experience. By continually enhancing programs, introducing new offerings based on member feedback and market trends, and proactively seeking member feedback, fitness studio owners can create an environment that keeps members engaged, motivated, and committed to their fitness journey.

Finally, it's important for fitness studio owners to stay up-to-date with industry trends, innovations, and evolving consumer expectations. Keeping a finger on the pulse of the industry through participation in conferences, educational programs, and networking events can provide valuable insights and foster professional development.

As fitness studio owners navigate the intricacies of the industry, it is clear that success lies in a combination of strategic planning, effective marketing, efficient operations, and a customer-centric approach. By focusing on these key areas, fitness studio owners can establish a thriving business that not only makes a positive impact on the lives of their members but also contributes to the overall health and well-being of the community they serve.

Made in the USA
Coppell, TX
11 December 2024

42297149R00049